Vintage Cleveland II
More Photographs of Yesteryear

by: James A. Toman

Gregory G. Deegan

Daniel J. Cook

Publishing Information

Published by
Cleveland Landmarks Press, Inc.
13610 Shaker Boulevard, Suite 503
Cleveland, Ohio 44120-1592
www.clevelandlandmarkspress.com
(216) 658 4144

©2012, Cleveland Landmarks Press, Inc.
All Rights Reserved

ISBN: 978-0-936760-33-9

Library of Congress Control Number: 2012910636

Designed by
John Yasenosky, III

Printed by:
Sheridan Books
Chelsea, Michigan

Table of Contents

Preface & Acknowledgments

It was three years ago that Cleveland Landmarks Press published a pictorial review of late 19th-early 20th Century Cleveland. Photos in the book were almost entirely from the extensive collection which the late Bruce Young had willed to the Special Collections division of Cleveland State University's Michael Schwartz Library. Bruce had operated a boutique called Photographs of Yesteryear, and that proved decisive in choosing a title for the review.

The book found a ready audience and sold out in a few years. A sizable segment of the Greater Cleveland community cares deeply about the city, and they showed a surprising interest in its history. Dialogue with purchasers of the first book revealed how fondly they recalled some other aspects of their hometown, and many inquired if the book contained images on those topics. Those inquiries whetted our research appetites and formed the basis for undertaking new searches into the archives for a *Vintage Cleveland* sequel. This volume, *Vintage Cleveland II, More Photographs of Yesteryear*, is the result.

Producing a book always involves more people than those whose names appear on the title page. Their help is truly the foundation in moving any project beyond its beginning outline to a finished product.

We are grateful to Bill Barrow and Lynn Duchez Bycko of the Special Collections Department of Cleveland State University's Michael Schwartz Library. Not only have they assembled an outstanding collection of Cleveland resource material, they are unfailingly helpful and gracious in making it available to the researcher.

We are also grateful to Margaret L. Baughman, photograph librarian at Cleveland Public Library, and to her staff members, Patrice Hamiter and Sabrina Miranda, for their kind and helpful service.

We thank John Yasenosky, III, for his patience in working with us, and even more so for the care and creativity he faithfully devotes to his task of designing our books. We also thank Alan Dutka, who so diligently markets our books, and Mike Miller and Marsha Clement for their promptly and efficiently distributing them to the vendors.

And, as always, we thank Kathy Cook and Liz Deegan for their unwavering support.

An Ever-changing Downtown

For more than 100,000 individuals, downtown Cleveland is their workplace. A similar number make the trek downtown for other reasons. Some visit the government and legal offices clustered in the city center. Some attend classes. And some seek diversion, visiting the museums; enjoying the theatre; rooting for the city's baseball, basketball, hockey, or football teams; or testing their luck at the casino.

These regular downtown visitors quickly become acclimated to the existing scene, which can seem unchanging. Even for those who have been involved in downtown Cleveland for decades and who have witnessed many changes, the present reality can erode memories of earlier days, making the current scene seem as though it were always in place. How many people today traveling along Ontario Street between Carnegie Avenue and Huron Road can recall the scene before Gateway got underway? Yet those sports venues have not yet begun their third decade.

Downtown is always changing, but in the second decade of the 21st Century it is experiencing a major makeover. The successful apartment projects that mark East Fourth Street and the Warehouse District have whetted the demand for even more downtown living space. Downtown has become a neighborhood. In fact, it is the only area in Cleveland that has witnessed population growth in the last decade. Long-dormant commercial properties are being converted to modern apartments, and new construction such as the Cleveland State University North Campus project are injecting new vitality to the city center.

"Big ticket" projects are also moving forward. The Flats East Bank project gives Cleveland its first new office tower since 1991, when the Key Tower opened. An adjoining hotel and shops will add to the complex. The Medical Mart and

Convention Center, and the Phase One Horseshoe Cleveland Casino in the Higbee Building will draw many visitors to Cleveland, which in turn will prompt additional demand for hotel rooms and corresponding amenities.

As gratifying as it may be to witness rehabilitation of older structures or construction of new facilities, it is intriguing to visualize what came earlier and important to remember them as part of another era in Cleveland's rich history. The images of an older Cleveland provide a meaningful timeline for urban change, and perhaps of equal importance, they can trigger poignant memories of formative and rewarding times.

Guarding the northeast quadrant of Public Square at Rockwell Avenue, the familiar Society for Savings Building stands next to the old Cleveland Chamber of Commerce Building. Designed by Peabody and Stearns, the neoclassical Chamber building was dedicated in 1899. In its final years, it served as the downtown home of Western Reserve University's Cleveland College. The building was razed in 1953, and its site became a parking lot for Society Bank. The city's tallest building, Key Tower, now occupies the site. *(Cleveland Public Library Cleveland Picture Collection)*

The photo above, taken from the 42nd floor observation deck of the Terminal Tower, provide dramatic evidence of the magnitude of change which has occurred in downtown Cleveland over the past 60 years. The views look towards the northeast. The top photo, taken in 1950, shows nothing of architectural note beyond East Sixth Street. (Jim Toman collection)
The view on the next page, taken in 2010, reveals the extent to which the skyline assumed a stunning new vertical profile. (Jim Toman photo)

For more than 75 years, the northwest quadrant of Public Square was bordered by the 1913 Marshall Building and the 1895 Mohawk Building. Between the two buildings *(left, Cleveland* Press *Collection of the Cleveland State University Michael Schwartz Library)* was a multi-story billboard typically garnished with a whiskey advertisement. In 1965, the Marshall Building, then named One Public Square Building, was expanded to fill the space once occupied by the billboard. It and its neighbor, then named the 33 Public Square Building, were refaced, giving them a modern appearance *(right, 1989 Jim Toman photo)*. Both buildings were razed in 1990 to make way for a new headquarters tower for Ameritrust Bank. Those plans were later dropped, and the site became a surface parking lot.

(Facing Page) Standing tall at the southeastern corner of Public Square in 1950 are the 16-story Williamson Building and its eight-story Cuyahoga Building neighbor. Designed by the prominent Chicago firm of Burnham and Root, the Cuyahoga Building opened in 1892. The 1900 Williamson Building, by George B. Post and Sons, was then the tallest building in the city.
(Cleveland Press Collection of the Cleveland State University Michael Schwartz Library)

(Left) The two buildings were imploded on October 3, 1982, to make way for a new home for the Standard Oil Company of Ohio (later a part of British Petroleum); The sign on the Williamson Building says "BOOM TIME."
(Standard Oil Company of Ohio photo, Jim Toman collection)

The Brotherhood of Locomotive Engineers Building, which fronted the southeast corner of St. Clair Avenue and Ontario Street, became the union's new home in 1909. The structure was built to the specifications of architects Knox and Elliot, who gave it a terra cotta finish to match that of its Standard Building neighbor. (*Cleveland* Press *Collection of the Cleveland State University Michael Schwartz Library*)

The Engineers Building was razed in 1989 to make way for the Society (Key) Center project. Today the Marriott Cleveland Downtown occupies the site. (*Jim Toman photo*)

The Bailey Company was one of downtown's six department stores. Incorporated in 1881, the store occupied the northeast corner of Ontario Street and Prospect Avenue. This view shows the store after 1910 when the original seven-story building was enlarged by a ten-story addition to the north. As shoppers abandoned downtown for more convenient suburban centers, Bailey's business began to lag. The store closed in March 1962. It was then razed, and the neighboring May Company erected its Parkade on the site. *(Cleveland Union Terminal Collection of the Cleveland State University Michael Schwartz Library)*

The Sterling and Welch Company, later one of the components of the consolidated Sterling Lindner Davis, was downtown's foremost home furnishing store. The Union Club is to its left *(Bruce Young Collection of the Cleveland State University Michael Schwartz Library).*

It was also the site of the famous Christmas tree which annually presided in the store's five-story atrium. This is the 1960 edition. (After Sterling Lindner Davis closed in December 1968, the atrium building was demolished to make way for a surface parking lot. *(Cleveland Press Collection of the Cleveland State University Michael Schwartz Library)*

The Cleveland *Press* called the northwest corner of East Ninth Street and Rockwell Avenue home until 1959. In that year, the newspaper moved to a new facility at the northeast corner of East Ninth Street and Lakeside Avenue. The paper's move and the influential voice of its editor, Louis B. Seltzer, played major roles in persuading the City of Cleveland to undertake the Erieview urban renewal project, which transformed the East Ninth Street-East 12th Street section of downtown Cleveland. The Press's old home was torn down in 1961.
(Cleveland Press *Collection of the Cleveland State University Michael Schwartz Library)*

The new Cleveland *Press* Building opened in 1959, and from that site served its afternoon readers until June 17, 1982 when it ceased publication. The paper had been in business for 104 years. The upper floors of the building were torn down, but its foundation was preserved as the lower level of the North Point 1 Building, today's home of the Jones Day law firm.
(Cleveland Press *Collection of the Cleveland State University Michael Schwartz Library)*

Until 1960, Cleveland's *Plain Dealer* operated from this building at the northwest corner of Superior Avenue and East Sixth Street. That year, the *Plain Dealer* moved to the former home of the Cleveland *News* at Superior Avenue and East 18th Street. Its old home became an annex to the downtown Cleveland Public Library. The annex was razed in 1994 to make way for the new Louis Stokes Wing, which opened in 1997. *(Jim Toman photo)*

The Penton Publishing Company, incorporated in 1904, moved into its new headquarters building on West Third Street at Lakeside Avenue in 1921. Cuyahoga County purchased the building site in 1971 to make way for construction of its new Justice Center. The Penton Building had been sturdily built to hold the heavy presses required by a printing company; the wreckers earned their pay during their laborious efforts to bring the structure down. Penton, a major publisher of trade journals, then moved to the Penton Plaza Building and currently occupies the former Bond Court Building on East Ninth Street, now renamed as the Penton Media Building. *(Cleveland* Press *Collection of the Cleveland State University Michael Schwartz Library)*

Its turrets gave the Central Armory the look of a medieval castle. Located on Lakeside Avenue and East Sixth Street, the armory was well known to Clevelanders because it hosted a large number of public events, especially gymnastics and boxing competitions.
In 1965, the Erieview urban renewal plan brought about the demolition of the 1893 building. Its site today is occupied by the Anthony J. Celebrezze Federal Office Building. *(Bruce Young Collection of the Cleveland State University Michael Schwartz Library)*

The Cuyahoga River

It was the confluence of the Cuyahoga River and Lake Erie that in 1796 convinced Moses Cleaveland and his band of explorers from the Connecticut Land Company that they had found an ideal location to build their new settlement. The town's location on the lake would serve well for transporting produce and raw materials back east, and the river would allow travel to the south. That inland route was greatly enhanced by the 1827 opening of the Ohio and Erie Canal, which had its northern terminus on the river at the foot of Superior Avenue

The Seneca Indians had given the river its name, "Cuyahoga" meaning "crooked," an apt name for its twisting and winding course. It was along this crooked river that Cleveland's industrial future began. Ongoing engineering made the river more navigable. In 1827 a new mouth for the river (its present location) shortened its route to Lake Erie. Subsequent reinforcement of its banks and dredging created a channel that would allow long bulk carriers to proceed farther upriver to directly serve the steel mills located there.

The Cuyahoga's usefulness to industry exacted a great price, its once pristine waters becoming toxic and foul-smelling as gasoline and other chemicals discarded by the plants emptied directly into the river. Its nadir came in June 22, 1969, when the Cuyahoga became the "burning river," its flames drawing national attention and making the city, then suffering from the "rustbelt syndrome," into a target for comedians' lampoons. It was not the first fire on the river, but it was the one that became the catalyst for major and ongoing cleanup projects.

Those environmental efforts have resulted in fish, birds, and other wildlife returning to the river. People also are now choosing the river for recreational pursuits. The Rivergate Park on the Columbus Road Peninsula has created a center for people interested in kayaking or row boating.

The Cuyahoga River still faces challenges. Bulkheads needs to be restored, and a new containment basin must be found for the material continually dredged from the river bottom. Yet today the river is healthier than at any time during the past century, and even as its recreational use burgeons, it continues its role as a critical link to Cleveland's vital steel-making center.

This photo clearly illustrates why the name "Cuyahoga" so well fits the river's twisting character. This 1964 view looks north towards Lake Erie. *(Cleveland* Press *Collection of the Cleveland State University Michael Schwartz Library)*

The iconic U. S. Coast Guard Station has stood at the mouth of the Cuyahoga River since 1940. Since 1976, when the Coast Guard relocated its headquarters to the foot of East Ninth Street, the river station has largely been vacant. It is now the property of the City of Cleveland.
(1950, Cleveland Press *Collection of the Cleveland State University Michael Schwartz Library)*

While it was the 1969 fire on the river that resulted in so public a response, fires were commonplace. Gasoline spills *(left, Cleveland* Press *Collection of the Cleveland State University Michael Schwartz Library)* and fires on the wooden docks that lined the river, made fireboats vital components in river safety management. *(right, Bruce Young Collection of the Cleveland State University Michael Schwartz Library)*

The crooked Cuyahoga made it difficult for large ore carriers to negotiate its turns. To aid in navigation, engineers broadened the channel (top center of photo). Greater Clevelanders know this as "collision bend." To the left of the photo are the former Cleveland Union Terminal coach yards. The scene is from 1948. *(Bruce Young Collection of the Cleveland State University Michael Schwartz Library)*

A boat of the Great Lakes Dredge and Dock Company cruises along the river in 1952. Founded in 1890, the Cleveland company played a major role in dredging operations and bulkhead upkeep along the Cuyahoga as well as in installation and repair of dock and breakwater facilities on the lakefront. *(Bruce Young Collection of the Cleveland State University Michael Schwartz Library)*

With a tug for guidance, a large ore carrier from the Cleveland-Cliffs fleet eases beneath the Detroit-Superior Bridge on its way upriver for unloading. *(Cleveland Press Collection of the Cleveland State University Michael Schwartz Library)*

City of Bridges

As important as the Cuyahoga River was to the commercial vitality of the 1796 settlement on Lake Erie, it also posed challenges that threatened future growth.

People settled both the east and west sides of the Cuyahoga. In March 1836, the settlement of those residing on the east side of the river was incorporated as Cleveland, while the western shore of the river was incorporated as Ohio City. The villages were politically distinct, and though they were connected by a floating Center Street Bridge, the two communities were more interested in gaining a competitive edge than in neighborly good relations.

The tension was most graphically demonstrated in the "Bridge War" of 1837. In that year Cleveland real estate promoters paid for construction of a Columbus Street Bridge. The bridge was located south of the Center Street Bridge, and likewise south of the Ohio City boundary. It meant that commerce could bypass the west side community. Cleveland then ordered the portion of the Center Street Bridge reaching the eastern edge of the river to be torn down. Tempers flared, and armed men from both sides of the river convened to take action. Gunshots were exchanged, and three citizens were wounded before the county sheriff broke up the fight. The court then ruled in favor of a two-bridge solution.

Cleveland's advantages were firmly rooted and its future dominance seemed unassailable. The competition finally came to an end in 1854 with Cleveland's annexation of Ohio City.

By then it had become clear to city leaders that the future growth and prosperity of the city depended on better cross-river access. The era of the big bridges was about to dawn.

In 1872 voters approved a bond issue for construction of the Superior Viaduct. The $2.2 million span would cross the river valley from Detroit Avenue and West 25th Street to Superior Avenue and West 10th Street. The bridge opened to traffic in December 1878.

While the Viaduct was a great improvement over the earlier river-level bridges that preceded it, the growth of vehicular traffic would soon demand an even better solution. More—and bigger—bridges were not long in following.

This view of the Superior Viaduct looks west. The western portion of the viaduct was built on stone arches which survive to the present. The girder-design of the eastern portion, which crossed the Cuyahoga River, featured a pivoting center draw which opened to allow tall ships to pass through. That feature resulted in delays for vehicular traffic and led to calls for a truly high level bridge to replace the viaduct. The viaduct opened to traffic in 1878 and closed in 1920. The eastern portion was torn down in 1922. *(Bruce Young Collection of the Cleveland State University Michael Schwartz Library)*

In 1934, a freighter passes beneath the Central Viaduct as a streetcar travels along its deck. The bridge, which opened to traffic in December 1888, connected Central Avenue (which then reached Ontario Street) to the west side at West 25th Street and Lorain Avenue. The viaduct was eventually superseded by the Lorain-Carnegie Bridge, and it was closed in 1941 and then demolished. (*Cleveland* Press *Collection of the Cleveland State University Michael Schwartz Library*)

This scene of the Central Viaduct looks toward the east. The Terminal Tower and Ohio Bell buildings can be seen in the distance. It is 1940, and the viaduct will soon face demolition. *(Cleveland* Press *Collection of the Cleveland State University Michael Schwartz Library)*

A series of bridges eases traffic over the rights of way for the CSX Railroad and the RTA Red Line Rapid Transit to Windermere. In the foreground the first bridge carries Buckeye Road traffic. The second carries Woodland Avenue over the tracks. It was the presence of this railroad corridor which determined the route for the eastern portion of the rapid transit line.
(Bruce Young Collection of the Cleveland State University Michael Schwartz Library)

The Detroit-Superior Bridge (now named the Veterans Memorial Bridge) was the city's first "high level" bridge. "High level," in this case 96 feet above the river, meant that the bridge would not have to open to let boats pass through. In 1916 erection of the bridge's 591-foot central arch is underway. The bridge was built with two levels. The bottom course was reserved for streetcars. *(Cuyahoga County Engineer's Collection of the Cleveland State University Michael Schwartz Library)*

In 1950 a streetcar rumbles across the lower deck of the Detroit-Superior Bridge on its way to the west side. Through the arch can be seen the stone superstructure of the former Superior Viaduct, and farther in the distance the deck of the Main Avenue Bridge. *(Herb Harwood photo)*

The Center Street swing bridge, one of several low-level bridges across the Cuyahoga River, opens to allow the *Goodtime* to pass through. *(Cleveland* Press *Collection of the Cleveland State University Michael Schwartz Library)*

The approaches to the Lorain-Carnegie Bridge are guarded by four pairs of 40-foot carved stone figures, known collectively as the Guardians of Traffic. Once threatened by a proposal of then-County Engineer Albert Porter, both the bridge and its sculptures gained protection by their inclusion on the National Register of Historic Places. *(Cuyahoga County Engineer's Collection of the Cleveland State University Michael Schwartz Library)*

The Lorain-Carnegie Bridge (renamed the Hope Memorial Bridge in 1983 to honor the stonemason heritage of comedian Bob Hope and his family) was the city's second high-level river crossing.   About 1,000 feet longer than the Detroit-Superior Bridge, the span connects the east side to Lorain Avenue near the West Side Market. The bridge was built with two decks, but the lower one was never completed. The bridge opened to traffic in November 1932. *(Cleveland Press Collection of the Cleveland State University Michael Schwartz Library)*

Because of its deteriorated condition, the Clark-Pershing Bridge, seen here when it was new in 1917, was closed to traffic in 1978. It was razed in two stages between 1981 and 1985.
(Cleveland Press *Collection of the Cleveland State University Michael Schwartz Library)*

In 1929 the Cuyahoga Viaduct is nearing completion. Part of the Cleveland Union Terminal project, it connected the station to the west side of the city. A Penn Central passenger train to Chicago was the last railroad use of the viaduct, but it remains in service as the Greater Cleveland Regional Transit Authority's Red Line link between downtown and Cleveland Hopkins International Airport.
(Cleveland Union Terminal Collection of the Cleveland State University Michael Schwartz Library)

The Sidaway Pedestrian Bridge, built in 1931, is the city's only suspension bridge. It was built to connect neighborhoods separated by Kingsbury Run. The bridge deck was partially removed in 1966, making the span no longer navigable. In this view, one can see the former shop and yard of the Shaker Heights Rapid Transit beneath the bridge. (*Cleveland* Press *Collection of the Cleveland State University Michael Schwartz Library*)

In 1933 the old Main Street Bridge is clogged with automobiles, a daily experience for commuters traveling between downtown and the west side. Built in 1886, the two-lane low-level swing bridge opened on average 28 times a day to allow the passage of river traffic, greatly contributing to traffic snarls. (*Cleveland* Press *Collection of the Cleveland State University Michael Schwartz Library*)

The Main Avenue Bridge (officially the Harold H. Burton Memorial Bridge), seen here under construction in 1938, connected the Memorial Shoreway West to downtown Cleveland and beyond to the eastern portion of the Shoreway which then stretched to East 55th Street. Its construction eliminated the major bottleneck for traffic trying to cross the Cuyahoga River on the old two-lane Main Street Bridge. The Main Avenue Bridge entered service in October 1939. *(Cuyahoga County Engineer's Collection of the Cleveland State University Michael Schwartz Library)*

The six-lane Main Avenue Bridge opened in 1939 and greatly eased east-west traffic in the city. It constituted the vital link across the Cuyahoga River as part of the city's first cross-town freeway, connecting the Memorial Shoreway West to downtown Cleveland and beyond to the eastern portion of the Shoreway which then stretched to East 55th Street. *(Cleveland* Press *Collection of the Cleveland State University Michael Schwartz Library)*

Bridges require continuous maintenance, but despite the best efforts, sometimes the pace of deterioration cannot be halted. Here in 1970, the old Harvard-Denison Bridge, whose traffic was already limited, carries a sign for motorists that only a single lane is open ahead. The bridge was torn down later that year; its replacement opened in 1978. *(Cleveland* Press *Collection of the Cleveland State University Michael Schwartz Library)*

The Innerbelt Bridge was the first project undertaken in constructing a freeway between the Memorial Shoreway and Interstate highways 71 and 90 to the south and west respectively. Work on the bridge began in 1954 and was completed in 1959.
(Cleveland Press *Collection of the Cleveland State University Michael Schwartz Library)*

This view of the Innerbelt Freeway and Bridge looks toward the west. The entire freeway project took eight years to build. The Lorain-Carnegie Bridge is to the right of the image. In 2012 work is underway to build a replacement for the aging Innerbelt span.
(Gerald Brookins Collection of the Cleveland State University Michael Schwartz Library)

Hotels of the Past

As a thriving commercial center, Cleveland was a major destination for the business traveler. The city was a headquarters city for many major industrial companies, as well as for the railroads, banks, and unions. As business representatives arrived at one of the city train stations, often after hours of travel, they were more than ready for a comfortable room and a good meal to prepare them for the next day's round of meetings.

Cleveland's prominence in the commercial world was also responsible for it becoming host city for conventions, and these brought visitors in numbers that made hotel proprietors gleeful. The influx of this strand of visitor compensated for times when occupancy rates were insufficient to cover the costs and generate a profit for the lodging operator.

A variety of hotel accommodations were ready to welcome all these visitors to town.

The importance of the hotels, however, was not limited to the traveler. Their meeting rooms and banquet facilities also served the local population. Hotels hosted all kinds of civic events and political forums. They were ideal settings for company celebrations and school reunions. Wedding receptions were another common event to utilize a hotel's hospitality services.

The chief hotels also boasted excellent kitchens, and their dining rooms were favorite locations for everything from hearty breakfasts and business lunches, to fine supper dining. All these features made the city's hotels familiar places to travelers and locals alike.

Hotels are particularly vulnerable to changing times. Accommodations need to keep pace with customer expectations. These in turn are greatly influenced by constantly changing trends in fashion and style.

Older hotels that couldn't keep pace with the changes lost their competitive edge, and newer venues took over the spotlight. Hotel ownership and management frequently changed, and after investment in renovation and modernization, older facilities often took on new names. Control readily passed back and forth between local proprietors and a series of national chains.

Cleveland's hotel scene has witnessed a great deal of change.

The Weddell House greeted its first guests in 1847. Originally built with a frontage along Superior Avenue at West Sixth Street, the hotel later added a wing facing West Sixth. The Superior Avenue portion of the hotel was razed in 1904 to make way for the Rockefeller Building. The remaining portion, as seen here in 1921, was demolished in 1961. Its site is now a parking lot.
(Cleveland Press *Collection of the Cleveland State University Michael Schwartz Library)*

The Forest City House on Public Square, an expanded version of the earlier Dunham House, opened in 1852. It was situated across from the pond that graced the southwest quadrant of the Square. Forest City House continued in business until 1915 when it was razed to make way for the Van Sweringens' Hotel Cleveland.
(Ohio Historical Society photo)

The Hawley House, at the corner of St. Clair Avenue and West Third Street, opened for business in 1882. It is seen here in 1974, hemmed in by the parking garage erected for the Illuminating Building in 1957. A residence hotel in its later years, the establishment was gutted by a fire in December 1974 and razed in 1975.
(Cleveland Press Collection of the Cleveland State University Michael Schwartz Library)

Born Hotel Winton in 1916, the property was renamed Hotel Carter in 1931. Located on Prospect Avenue, just east of East Ninth Street, it later became the Pick Carter. After being converted to apartments in 1972, it was renamed the Carter Manor. Following a complete renovation, in 2006 the building returned to its original name and is now known as the Winton Manor.
(1947, Cleveland Picture Collection of Cleveland Public Library)

The vintage hotel gave way to a new version, the Hollenden House, in 1965. The Hollenden House, however, only lasted until 1989, when it too was razed. The Hollenden site is now home to today's Fifth-Third Tower.
(Cleveland Press Collection of the Cleveland State University Michael Schwartz Library)

Hotel Hollenden opened its doors to the public in 1885. Located on the southeast corner of Superior Avenue and East Sixth Street, the 700-room hotel was the city's largest and most modern, and its Vogue Room remained a popular watering hole for years.
(1947, Cleveland Press Collection of the Cleveland State University Michael Schwartz Library).

The intersection of Euclid Avenue, Huron Road, and East 14th Street hosted a hotel from 1874 until 1940. In that year the Hotel Euclid gave way to a smaller building which eventually became home to the Black Angus and later to the Rusty Scupper and Sweetwater Cafe restaurants. The corner is now the site of the regional headquarters building for US Bank. *(Cleveland Picture Collection of Cleveland Public Library)*

The Allerton Hotel made its debut in November 1926. Situated at the corner of East 13th Street (left) and Chester Avenue, the hotel was known for its variety of exercise and fitness facilities. The Allerton was later taken over by the Manger hotel chain, and then was converted to apartments under the Parkview name. In 2010, after a renovation, it was renamed the Allerton Apartments. *(1947, Cleveland Press Collection of the Cleveland State University Michael Schwartz Library)*

A streetcar passes Hotel Auditorium, at the northeast corner of St. Clair Avenue and East Sixth Street. Built in 1927, the 200-room hotel was situated to take advantage of its proximity to Cleveland Public Auditorium and Music Hall, just across East Sixth Street. Falling within the Erieview urban renewal boundaries, it closed in July 1969 and was then demolished to make way for a new hotel as part of the Bond Court development. The replacement Bond Court Hotel opened in 1975, operating later under Sheraton and Crowne Plaza, and presently Westin management. *(Cleveland Press Collection of the Cleveland State University Michael Schwartz Library)*

The Hotel Statler Building, at Euclid Avenue and East 12th Street, has worn many faces since it first opened in 1912. The 1,000-room hotel and its popular Terrace Room restaurant became the Statler Hilton in 1954, then the Cleveland Plaza in 1973. In 1980, the hotel was converted to offices and known as the Statler Office Tower. In 2002 it was renovated once again, this time emerging as the Statler Arms Apartments. The view is of the main entrance to the Statler in 1937. (*Cleveland* Press *Collection of the Cleveland State University Michael Schwartz Library*)

The Olmsted Hotel occupied the northwest corner of Superior Avenue and East Ninth Street. Opened in 1916, it continued as a hotel until 1964, when new owners gave the building a modern exterior appearance and turned its 293 guest rooms into 116 apartments. It also received a new name, The Regency.
(Cleveland *Press* Collection of the Cleveland State University Michael Schwartz Library)

The Regency continued as an apartment building until 1996 when it was torn down to make way for construction of a new Hampton Inn. The new hotel opened in 1998. This view is from 1995. *(Jim Toman photo)*

Located at the eastern fringe of the downtown area, Euclid Avenue and East 22nd Street, Hotel New Amsterdam opened to the public in 1902. It continued until 1969 when it was razed to make way for a new Holiday Inn, which registered its first guests in 1972. In 1986, the property was purchased by Cleveland State University, and the Inn became the Viking Hall dormitory. It was torn down in 2012 to create room for a new campus Science Center.
(Cleveland Press Collection of the Cleveland State University Michael Schwartz Library)

Fine Dining & Fast Food

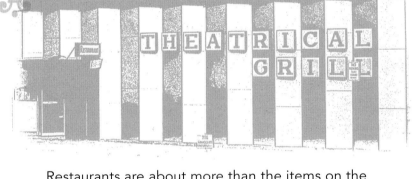

Food preferences change with time, and so too do the purveyors. Restaurants live a rather ephemeral existence. Today's dining hotspots often quickly become yesterday's story.

In the late 1980s a new Cleveland poster made its appearance. It was entitled "Cleveland Lights." On it were images of the complimentary matchbooks that were offered to guests from 35 popular Cleveland area restaurants. Restaurant matchbooks themselves have become a thing of the past, a clear sign of changing values and habits.

More to the point, a quarter century after that poster made its debut, only eight of the 35 restaurants depicted on it remain in business. Some are gone because their owners no longer were willing to continue the demanding work which restaurant management requires. Others closed because landlords terminated leases. Others faded from the scene as customers abandoned their old favorites for some of the newer palate pleasers that came into being.

And yet, it is common for thoughts of yesterday's restaurants to bring back warm and satisfying memories.

Restaurants are about more than the items on the menu. Their ambiance often captured a mood as much as their food satisfied an appetite. Restaurants were often the places where diners celebrated special events in their lives. And maybe most importantly, it was to the accompaniment of dinner and drinks that many of one's most poignant conversations took place.

New restaurants are constantly popping up, and diners typically like to give them a trial. Yet a look at some of those old favorites, now faded from the scene, should surely cook up some meaningful memories.

The Forum Cafeteria, located in the Rose Building on East Ninth Street between Prospect and Euclid avenues, was a popular lunch spot. Part of a national chain, the Forum served Cleveland customers from 1931 until 1983.
(*Cleveland* Press *Collection of the Cleveland State University Michael Schwartz Library*)

Mills Restaurant was located at 315 Euclid Avenue. Many Clevelanders fondly remember the large windmill sign affixed on the front of the building. The popular cafeteria-style eatery claimed that with 650 seats, it was the largest dining space in the city. It served customers from 1919 until 1971. This postcard view shows its spacious interior.
(Walter Leedy Collection of the Cleveland State University Michael Schwartz Library)

Two women picket the Pickwick Cafeteria on lower Superior Avenue in 1941. They are seeking union recognition. The Pickwick had just moved to this site from its former location in the Arcade.
(Cleveland Press Collection of the Cleveland State University Michael Schwartz Library)

The Blue Boar Cafeteria, at 643 Euclid Avenue, was new to Cleveland in this 1935 scene. Part of a Louisville, Kentucky, restaurant chain, the Blue Boar remained in operation until 1955, when its space was taken over by the locally owned Pickwick Cafeteria.
(Cleveland Press *Collection of the Cleveland State University Michael Schwartz Library)*

It was hard to beat the view diners enjoyed at Jim's Steak House. Because it was situated on Scranton Road at the Cuyahoga River's Collision Bend, with a wonderful view of river traffic and the skyline beyond, Jim's created a dining experience that was truly special. Jim's opened in 1930 and continued in business until 1997. A few other proprietors later operated from the building which was razed in 2011.
(Cleveland Press Collection of the Cleveland State University Michael Schwartz Library)

Clark's Colonial at 1007 Euclid Avenue was one of 20 restaurants in the locally owned Clark chain. It opened in 1935. The Clark name, service, and famous apple pie remained on the scene until 1966.
(*Bruce Young Collection of the Cleveland State University Michael Schwartz Library*)

Captain Frank's Lobster House, at the foot of the East Ninth Street pier, was a popular dining spot for Clevelanders from 1954 until 1989. The restaurant building was demolished in 1994 to make way for lakefront improvements.
(*Cleveland* Press *Collection of the Cleveland State University Michael Schwartz Library*)

Perhaps it was as much the cheerful beer hall music as the weinerschnitzel that made Kiefer's a popular restaurant for almost half a century. Located on Detroit Avenue, just west of West 25th Street, the restaurant was originally known as the Schwarzwald, but its too-German name was replaced during World War II. The restaurant continued in business until 1991. *(Walter Leedy Collection of the Cleveland State University Michael Schwartz Library)*

Operated by the Weinberger family, Kornman's Restaurant, on East Ninth Street at Vincent Avenue, with a "Back Room" and entrance from Vincent, was a favorite dining and entertainment spot for Clevelanders and out-of-town visitors. It continued in business until 1967 when its site was cleared to make way for the new headquarters building of Central National Bank. The scene here is from 1960. *(Cleveland Press Collection of the Cleveland State University Michael Schwartz Library)*

For 70 years Kluck's Restaurant on West 117th Street served up German and fish favorites to its loyal clientele. With its pine-paneled dining room and its nautical décor, Kluck's was a particular favorite for business lunches. Kluck's closed in 2007, but its largely unchanged dining room is now home to a Mexican restaurant. (*Cleveland* Press *Collection of the Cleveland State University Michael Schwartz Library*)

Playhouse Square was well suited to the restaurant business, and the corner of East 14th Street and Euclid Avenue at Huron Road was the site for a succession of eateries. The Black Angus occupied the spot from 1955 to 1972. It was followed by the Rusty Scupper from 1976 to 1984 and the Sweetwater Café from 1984 to 1988. Construction of the Renaissance Building (now the US Bank Center) in 1988 ended the restaurant reign. (*Jim Toman photo*)

The New York Spaghetti House, with its famous brown sauce, was a long-time Cleveland favorite. Located on East Ninth Street, across from today's Progressive Field, the Italian eatery opened for business in 1927. It closed in 2001, but under new management reopened from 2004 to 2007. This postcard view shows the downstairs dining room. *(Walter Leedy Collection of the Cleveland State University Michael Schwartz Library)*

Stouffer's Restaurant at 725 Euclid Avenue was actually the fourth location for the firm's original eatery which had opened in the Arcade in 1922. This Euclid Avenue location opened in 1940. The restaurant ran from Euclid Avenue to Short Vincent Street, and diners could enter or leave from either portal. Sometimes those who had entered from Euclid Avenue and had enjoyed a sedate Stouffer's dinner might look for a more lively conclusion to their evening. The Vincent exit made for ready access to the varied entertainment along Vincent's gaudy stretch. *(Cleveland Press Collection of the Cleveland State University Michael Schwartz Library)*

Stouffer's Restaurant, on the first floor of the Stouffer Corporation headquarters building, was a mainstay in Playhouse Square from 1936 until 1972. With the Square's theatres shuttered, the evening dinner trade dried up, and the restaurant closed. The building is now home to Ideastream, the broadcasting center for WVIZ, WCPN, and WCLV.
(Cleveland Transit System photo, Jim Toman collection)

Pat Joyce's Tavern on East Ninth Street was a bustling place at lunch time. The restaurant was located on the first floor of the Ellington Apartments building. The site was cleared in 1967 to make way for the Central National Bank office tower.
(Cleveland Picture Collection of Cleveland Public Library)

For more than a half century after its opening in 1937, the Theatrical Grill at 711 Vincent Avenue was probably Cleveland's most lively and lore-rich dining and watering spot. The view here is of the Theatrical in 1960 shortly before it was gutted by fire. It was totally rebuilt and went on for another 30 years entertaining customers with its jazz and generous drinks. *(Cleveland Picture Collection of Cleveland Public Library)*

Certainly not comparable to downtown's dining spots, Manner's Big Boy restaurants nonetheless struck a responsive chord with Clevelanders during the 1950s and 1960s. While Big Boy did offer indoor dining, ordering food from the car and having it delivered by "car hops" became a ritual for teenagers. This scene shows the drive-in area of the Mayfield Road Big Boy. *(Cleveland* Press *Collection of the Cleveland State University Michael Schwartz Library)*

The trademark "big boy" statue was once a familiar scene in Greater Cleveland, a welcoming figure to the Big Boy restaurants that dotted the area. The scene here is of the Big Boy training center on Euclid Avenue. By 2012, only two of the figures remained in the region to greet guests. *(Cleveland* Press *Collection of the Cleveland State University Michael Schwartz Library)*

Groceries & Supermarkets

While restaurants certainly possess a kind of appeal, for most folks dining out was the exception. Dining in – the home-cooked meal – was the rule. Over time, securing food for family fare, a major demand on time and the purse, has undergone significant change.

The popularity of today's community gardens recalls a time when many folks cultivated patches to grow vegetables. Such staples as potatoes, carrots, onions, green peppers, and zucchini were frequently home grown. Tomato vines were everywhere.

Fruit trees were also cultivated. If a person had sufficient space, his yard could contain apple, pear, plum, and cherry trees. Grape vines were also common.

Many folks also raised poultry, so eggs and chicken became staples on the kitchen table. The garden culture was strengthened by the exigencies of the Great Depression and then by the patriotic Victory Gardens popular during the World War II years.

Many food products, however, demanded more preparation time and/or skill than the homeowner could readily undertake, and so the neighborhood grocery store filled that need. Most groceries were small family-run establishments, often built onto the front of one's residence. Because of their size, the range of boxed, bagged, and canned items, as well as the fresh meats and dairy products stocked in their coolers was limited.

Finding items not carried at the corner grocery usually meant a trip to one of Cleveland's large central markets. The Sheriff Street, Central, and Westside markets were packed with fresh produce, meats, and prepared food items.

The passage of the years and expanded range for shopping made possible by the family car made larger stores—supermarkets—practical. Because their size and corresponding purchase power allowed the supermarkets to sell food at lower prices than the neighborhood grocery, the local stores could no longer compete. Slowly they went the way of such predecessors as the trading post and general store.

The grocery chains themselves, both national and local, have come and gone. Cleveland today is served by two local supermarket companies, Heinen's and Dave's, as well as by a number of national outfits.

Today super-stores, carrying everything from hardware, to clothing, to home furnishings, as well as groceries, are making inroads on the supermarkets. The food industry continues to evolve.

This 1940 scene of Pekarek's grocery store on Libby Road in Maple Heights captures the essence of the neighborhood market. The boy's bicycle out front probably meant that he had been dispatched by his mother to get a few items for that day's supper. The neighborhood stores made shopping convenient. *(Cleveland Press Collection of the Cleveland State University Michael Schwartz Library)*

While the neighborhood grocery offered convenience to shoppers, it also was vulnerable to crime. Small and with usually only one person on duty, the grocery store was an inviting target for robbers. Although the Townsels tried hard to maintain their East 123rd Street store, three robberies prompted them to give up on their dream. The store closed in 1967.
(*Cleveland* Press *Collection of the Cleveland State University Michael Schwartz Library*)

Fisher Brothers was the Cleveland area's largest chain of grocery stores from 1907 until 1965. It was renamed Fisher Foods in 1937, the new name appearing on its dignified store in the Shaker Square shopping center.
(Cleveland Press Collection of the Cleveland State University Michael Schwartz Library)

The brightly lighted store front and the light beacon above the store made the Fisher Foods store on Lee and Silsby roads in Cleveland Heights hard to miss. The scene is from 1939. *(Cleveland* Press *Collection of the Cleveland State University Michael Schwartz Library)*

In 1966 Fisher Foods is about to open a new store on Fulton Road. The Fisher chain was acquired in 1965 by another local company, and its stores would soon be bearing the Fazio name. *(Cleveland* Press *Collection of the Cleveland State University Michael Schwartz Library)*

The Pick-n-Pay supermarket chain began in 1925. An attractive marketing tool was awarding customers Eagle trading stamps. The stamps could be redeemed for merchandise at The May Company. Pictured here in 1956 is the Pick-n-Pay store in the Harvard-Lee Shopping center. (*Cleveland* Press *Collection of the Cleveland State University Michael Schwartz Library*)

The Pick-n-Pay store in Mapletown Shopping Center opened in 1947. The locally owned Pick-n-Pay chain was later sold and operated under the Finast and then Tops banners. The view here is from 1958.
(*Cleveland* Press *Collection of the Cleveland State University Michael Schwartz Library*)

The Stop-n-Shop name was a familiar presence in the Greater Cleveland community until 1998 when the local chain was purchased by nationally based Giant Eagle. In 1965 Stop-n-Shop celebrated the opening of its "country store" in Brecksville.
(*Cleveland* Press *Collection of the Cleveland State University Michael Schwartz Library*)

Stop-n-Shop used the St. Patrick's Day holiday to launch its new store on Broadview Road in 1976.
Owned by Riser Foods, a name drawn from the Rini, Rego, and Seaway companies which merged
to form it, the Stop-n-Shop chain once operated 34 stores in the Greater Cleveland area.
(Cleveland Press Collection of the Cleveland State University Michael Schwartz Library)

The Kroger Company, the nation's largest grocery chain, operated in the Greater Cleveland area until the mid-1980s when it withdrew from the local market. Here in 1956, it celebrates a new store on Buckeye Avenue near East 90th Street. That store later became a Bi-Rite market. It was razed in 2011.
(Cleveland Picture Collection of Cleveland Public Library)

Hough Bakeries was the Cleveland area's largest baked goods company, with 32 stores of its own as well as renting counter space in other business settings. Hough also ran a successful catering service. Here its store on Prospect Avenue continues in business even though its neighboring Taylor department store has been shuttered. *(Cleveland Picture Collection of Cleveland Public Library)*

The appealing display cases of Hough breads and sweet treats created a hard-to-resist temptation for the Cleveland shopper. While the area had several bakery chains as well as many small neighborhood ethnic bake shops, Hough's became the city's favorite, and it remains fondly remembered decades after its 1992 business closure.
(Cleveland Picture Collection of Cleveland Public Library)

Movie Theatres

It is a part of the human condition for people to seek at least occasional diversion from their daily concerns and duties. Clevelanders frequently turned to the theatre as their retreat from the mundane.

The legitimate theatre, of course, preceded the film palaces that would appear in the 20th Century. Prominent among these showplaces were the Academy of Music on West Sixth Street (1859), the Euclid Avenue Opera House on East Fourth Street (1875), and the Lyceum Theatre on Public Square (1883). Then in 1907 came the new Hippodrome Theatre, with entrances from both Euclid and Prospect avenues at about East Eighth Street. With over 3,500 seats, the theatre also boasted the city's largest stage.

The development of the "motion picture" and its climb to the summit of the entertainment world can probably be dated to the 1903 debut of *The Great Train Robbery*. Though only 12 minutes in length, it was the precursor of an entertainment mode that would reign supreme until the arrival of television.

The first movie theatres were located downtown. The Stillman Theatre, on Euclid Avenue, just west of Playhouse Square, was the first to be built specifically as a movie house. It opened in 1916. In 1927 it was also the first to screen a "talkie," *The Jazz Singer*. Euclid Avenue was Cleveland's "Movie Row." As late as 1950, in the stretch of Euclid Avenue between Public Square and Playhouse Square, 10 different theatres were presenting films.

The popularity of movies made it inevitable that they would be screened in neighborhood theatres across the city and the suburbs. In June 1950, newspaper display ads show that 81 Greater Cleveland theatres were operating. With the advent of television, however, the number of movie houses began to dwindle. By June 1960 the number had slipped to 49. There were also 8 drive-in theatres operating that same year.

Over time the single-screen neighborhood theatres gave

way to the multi-screen complexes. In 2012 there are 17 multi-plexes in the Greater Cleveland area, with the number of screens ranging from three to 24. Cuyahoga County no longer has any drive-in theatres.

Originally built for vaudeville, the Hippodrome Theatre, at 720 Euclid Avenue, also hosted orchestra concerts, grand opera, and stage plays. In 1931, it was remodeled to better accommodate motion pictures. With 4,100 seats, management at the "Hipp" (as it was nicknamed) claimed it as the second largest theatre in the world. The Hippodrome went dark in 1980 and was razed one year later. (*Cleveland* Press *Collection of the Cleveland State University Michael Schwartz Library*)

The Stillman Theatre, on Euclid Avenue just west of East 12th Street, was the first of the major downtown theatres to close. The end came in July 1963 after the theatre had completed its exclusive first-run presentation of *Lawrence of Arabia*. The theatre's auditorium was torn down and replaced by a parking garage. Entrance to the garage is through the theatre's former lobby. In this 1955 scene, a line of antique autos parades by.
(Cleveland Press *Collection of the Cleveland State University Michael Schwartz Library)*

In 1948 the new Mayland Theatre, on Mayfield Road in Mayfield Heights, is about to open. The Art Deco structure, with a huge auditorium, continued as a movie house until 1990 when it was remodeled into a large Barnes & Noble book store. In 2012 it houses a Boneyard restaurant.
(Cleveland Press Collection of the Cleveland State University Michael Schwartz Library)

The Olympia Theatre, on East 55th Street at Broadway Avenue, benefited from its proximity to the concentration of stores at the busy intersection as well as from its location on three major public transit routes. A streetcar passes the theatre early in 1953.
(Bruce Young Collection of the Cleveland State University Michael Schwartz Library)

The Doan Theatre, built in 1919 on St. Clair Avenue and East 105th Street, was one of the early movie houses to go dark. Here in 1958, its paint peeling, the theatre's auditorium is being used for a Sunday church service.
(Cleveland Press *Collection of the Cleveland State University Michael Schwartz Library)*

In 1961 Lakewood's Detroit Theatre was prospering. It outlasted many of the area's other neighborhood movie venues, continuing as a twin-screen theatre until 2011. The building was razed in 2012 to make way for a MacDonald's restaurant.
(Cleveland Press *Collection of the Cleveland State University Michael Schwartz Library)*

The Mercury Theatre on Pearl Road in Middleburg Heights, opened to the public in 1950. The original 1,400 seat auditorium was later converted into two smaller viewing areas. The Mercury closed in the early 1990s and was razed in 1994.
(Cleveland Press *Collection of the Cleveland State University Michael Schwartz Library)*

When the Park Centre apartment complex, between Superior and Chester avenues at East 12th and East 13th streets, opened in 1969, it was home to a two-screen cinema. The scene dates from 1974. The complex is now known as Reserve Square, and the former cinema space has been converted into studios for the WUAB and WOIO television stations. *(Cleveland Press Collection of the Cleveland State University Michael Schwartz Library)*

As attendance declined at the neighborhood movie houses, some operators sold their properties for other uses, often as church venues, while others, moving in a rather contrary direction, tried to hang on by showing adult films. That latter was the fate of the Lyceum Theatre on Fulton Road, seen here in 1980. *(Cleveland Press Collection of the Cleveland State University Michael Schwartz Library)*

The Roxy Theatre on East Ninth Street, between Euclid Avenue and Short Vincent Street, was Cleveland's longest-lasting burlesque house. Near its end, it primarily showed x-rated movies. The Roxy closed in November 1977. It was then razed to make way for the National City Bank (now PNC) headquarters project.
(Jim Toman photo)

The movie drive-ins showed considerable traction during the 1950s and 1960s. They took advantage of the dual appeal of both film and cars. Drive-ins had the added allure of offering young couples a relatively private venue to explore their relationships. Seen here is the Memphis Drive-In. By 2012 all the drive-ins had disappeared from Cuyahoga County.
(Cleveland Press Collection of the Cleveland State University Michael Schwartz Library)

Great Lakes Exposition

While many Greater Clevelanders struggled mightily through the Great Depression, the Great Lakes Exposition, held in the summers of 1936 – 1937, provided them the opportunity to focus, at least briefly, their attention on more positive developments. During the two summer seasons, more than seven million visitors took in the popular attractions, which were designed to feature the heady achievements of Cleveland and the Midwest over the previous century.

Hatched as an idea by Frank J. Ryan, Cleveland Electric Illuminating Company executive, and Lincoln J. Dickey, the city's first Public Hall commissioner, the sprawling display was an achievement unto itself. The Exposition encompassed approximately 135 acres, stretching from West 3rd to East 20th streets. Most activity centered around East 9th, the Mall, Public Auditorium, and Cleveland Municipal Stadium, which had been completed only five years earlier.

Organized to celebrate the centennial year of the City of Cleveland's incorporation, the festival featured hundreds of attractions, including rides, shows, and cafes. A "Streets of the World" promenade featured 200 cafes and bazaars with international flavors, a midway offered rides and sideshows, and a "Hall of Progress" highlighted developments that emerged from Cleveland ingenuity. Companies founded in Cleveland, such as Standard Oil, the White Motor Company, and Sherwin-Williams paraded their products and successes. The Marine Theater, in 1937 named Billy Rose's Aquacade, proved especially popular. Outside the building, powerful moving light beams recreated the Aurora Borealis lights. Inside, patrons enjoyed dinner and shows featuring water ballet, dancers, and even a model military boat parade. In addition, the 1937 season starred Eleanor Holm and Johnny Weismuller.

The Donald Gray Gardens, planted and arranged on three-and-a-half acres just north of Cleveland Municipal Stadium, remained the lone physical reminder of Cleveland's Depression-era show until the late 1990s, when the gardens were excavated to make way for construction of the new Cleveland Browns Stadium.

Planners created in the summers of 1936 and 1937 a huge festival that celebrated Cleveland, the Great Lakes, and their role in industrial progress. The Exposition sat near five-year-old Cleveland Municipal Stadium (to the northwest), East Ninth street (to the northeast), City Hall (to the southeast), and the County Court House (to the southwest). (*Cleveland* Press *Collection of the Cleveland State University Michael Schwartz Library*)

The Great Lakes Exposition transformed the downtown lakefront and the Group Plan mall. Covering approximately 135 acres, it stretched from West 3rd to East 20th streets and from the lakefront to St. Clair Avenue. The Court of Presidents bridged the mall area to the lakefront over the railroad tracks.
(*Cleveland* Press *Collection of the Cleveland State University Michael Schwartz Library*)

The main intersection of the Exposition united the area on the west side of the massive Automotive Building (top), the Standard Drug Company Building (bottom right, on the east side of the Court of Presidents), the Exposition cafeteria (bottom), and the Christian Science Building (top left). The Marine Plaza featured tended green space throughout the walkway. (*Cleveland* Press *Collection of the Cleveland State University Michael Schwartz Library*)

If patrons entered through the main entrance on Mall B, the bandshell framing the stage of the Sherwin-Williams Plaza would have greeted them. This view, looking northwest, shows the County Court House and Cleveland Municipal Stadium in the background. (*Cleveland* Press *Collection of the Cleveland State University Michael Schwartz Library*)

One of the main buildings in the Exposition was the Automotive Building, which featured 32 pylons, each stretching
70 feet into the sky, surrounding the structure. This view looks west, with Cleveland Municipal Stadium in the background.
(*Cleveland* Press *Collection of the Cleveland State University Michael Schwartz Library*)

A landscaped walkway along East Ninth framed the east side of the Automotive Building, which exhibited, according to the Exposition's souvenir booklet, "the most advanced contributions of the great automotive industries." (*Cleveland* Press *Collection of the Cleveland State University Michael Schwartz Library*)

Donald Gray, a gardening columnist for the Cleveland *Press*, helped design the gardens north of the recently constructed Cleveland Municipal Stadium. This view is north of Cleveland Municipal Stadium, looking west.
(*Cleveland* Press *Collection of the Cleveland State University Michael Schwartz Library*)

The Horticulture Building, a three-story building with three separate levels of outdoor terraces, resided just east of the gardens. East of that, the Aquacade and Marine Theater's shows – easily some of the most popular attractions – dazzled patrons.
(*Great Lakes Exposition of the Cleveland State University Michael Schwartz Library*)

The end of East Ninth Street featured one of Rear Admiral Richard E. Byrd's two ships that he took to the Antarctic between 1928 - 1930. Festival goers could board Byrd's Flagship, *The City of New York*, which had gained fame as a ship known in 1912 as the Samson, which was in the vicinity when the Titanic sunk. *(Cleveland* Press *Collection of the Cleveland State University Michael Schwartz Library)*

The Court of the Presidents bridged the mall area to the lakefront and connected the attractions on the lakefront such as the Donald Gray Gardens and the Automotive Building to those on the mall, such as the Sherwin-Williams Plaza. Designers surmounted huge eagles atop 16 of the booths along the Court to highlight the 16 presidents who had been born in or elected from a Great Lakes state. This view is looking north with the Automotive Building in the background. (*Cleveland* Press *Collection of the Cleveland State University Michael Schwartz Library*)

The Airports

Cuyahoga County is home to three airports: Cleveland Hopkins International Airport in the southwest corner of the city, Burke Lakefront Airport downtown, and Cuyahoga County Airport in the eastern suburbs.

Cleveland Hopkins was established in 1925 under the leadership of Cleveland's William R. Hopkins, who served as city manager from 1924-1933. It was the first municipal airport in the country. It achieved other firsts as well: first control tower, first radio communications between the tower and aircraft, and first night lighting for the field. In 1968 it became the first airport in the country to be connected to its downtown by rail rapid transit.

Between 1929 and 1949, the airport hosted the National Air Races, interrupted during the World War II years, twelve times.

During the first decade of the 21st Century, on average, Hopkins handled about 10 million annual passengers. It is served by nine airlines and is a regional hub to United Airlines.

Burke Lakefront Airport, named in honor of Thomas A. Burke, Cleveland mayor from 1946 to 1953, made its debut in 1947. It was conceived as a relief airport to Hopkins, and at the same time a practical use for the unattractive landfill that marked the city's lakefront. Its downtown location seemed to make Burke ideal for the business traveler. Over time, the role of the airport has evolved. Commercial service has been intermittent. Burke is now focused on serving private, business, and chartered aircraft. Burke has also been home to the Memorial Day weekend Grand Prix and the Labor Day weekend Air Show.

Cuyahoga County Airport, located off Richmond Road in Richmond Heights and Highland Heights, had its beginning as a private airfield in 1928, but it lay fallow after 1930. It was not until the county purchased the property in 1946 that significant progress was made towards developing the site as an airport facility. The airport was dedicated in 1950 and has been expanded both as an airfield for private and business aircraft and as a site for an office and industrial park.

This 1955 view of Cleveland Hopkins International Airport shows the new terminal as well as the original terminal building to its left. A less complicated world in those days, visitors were allowed to walk out on the concourse to watch planes land and take off.
(Cleveland Press *Collection of the Cleveland State University Michael Schwartz Library)*

In 1961, Hopkins has added a second concourse. The lower portion of the scene shows the large surface parking lot that preceded the short- and long-term garages that now grace the eastern front of the terminal building. The view looks toward the west.
(Cleveland Press *Collection of the Cleveland State University Michael Schwartz Library)*

The sculpture, Global Flight and Celebration, by C. E. Van Duzer, was installed at Hopkins in 1976 to mark the airport's 50th anniversary. (*Cleveland* Press *Collection of the Cleveland State University Michael Schwartz Library*)

United Airlines jets dominate the gates of Concourse C in 1978. Built in 1968, Concourse C, with 26 gates, is the largest of Hopkins' four passenger boarding/deplaning areas. (*Cleveland* Press *Collection of the Cleveland State University Michael Schwartz Library*)

For many years the lakefront east of East Ninth Street was the site of a dump. Smoke from burning debris wafted throughout the downtown area. That would finally change for the better with the establishment of Burke Lakefront Airport in 1947.
(Cleveland Press *Collection of the Cleveland State University Michael Schwartz Library)*

This 1960 view of the lakefront shows two short runways in place as well as the footprint for extending them to the east. It also shows how continuing landfill operations expanded the Burke site. *(Cleveland* Press *Collection of the Cleveland State University Michael Schwartz Library)*

By 1978 a terminal building and air traffic tower gave Burke Lakefront Airport the look of an active airfield. For several years the second floor of the terminal was the scene of a restaurant, from which diners could view activity on the runways below. *(Cleveland* Press *Collection of the Cleveland State University Michael Schwartz Library)*

This early aerial view of what would become Cuyahoga County Airport, when it was still a privately owned site, shows a hanger building on the cleared property. Change would begin to happen only after the county took ownership of the plot.
(Cleveland Press *Collection of the Cleveland State University Michael Schwartz Library)*

Signs of development mark the County Airport site in 1949. It would be dedicated one year later. Richmond Road is in the foreground.
(Cleveland Press *Collection of the Cleveland State University Michael Schwartz Library)*

A more modern view of the county airfield shows developed runways, hangers, and support buildings. The proximity of the airport to residential developments (bottom and to upper right) has spurred continuing opposition to the location of the airport and of its continued operation. (*Cleveland* Press *Collection of the Cleveland State University Michael Schwartz Library*)

Favorite Stores of Yesteryear

For persons of a certain age, the first thing that comes to mind when the topic is "stores," is the wonderful world of Cleveland's downtown department stores. Those too young to remember them missed a grand era of shopping. It was a time marked by copious choices of merchandise across a broad spectrum of clothing, furnishings, house wares, and accessories, offered in a range of prices, all presented in appealing and tasteful displays, in stores which were themselves elegantly designed.

The downtown department stores are all gone. Taylor's was the first to close, in 1961, followed by Bailey's in 1962, Sterling's in 1968, Halle's in 1982, May's in 1992, and Higbee/Dillard's in 2002. The May Company's suburban stores survived, but became known as Kaufmann's and then Macy's. The Higbee name disappeared from marquees in 1992, but the renamed Dillard stores continue in the suburbs. The downtown department store era is now only a memory.

Besides the department stores, many other establishments familiar to Clevelanders have also disappeared. A changing demographic, a different life style, and an evolving business model accounts for much of this.

Many locally owned stores were purchased by national companies, and whereas local roots at one time preserved only marginal operations, for the conglomerates the bottom line is what mattered most.

In the years following World War II, ever fewer people used public transportation to do their shopping. The primacy of the private automobile and the corresponding need for stores to have convenient parking put landlocked stores at a distinct competitive disadvantage.

The arrival of big box specialty stores redirected shoppers' buying habits. Instead of going to a store which carried only a limited selection of the commodity that the shopper was interested in, the stores that specialized in that kind of item (e.g., toys) did so with a much larger range of choices. This appeal was quite effective.

Regardless of the reason why the store scene has changed so much, for the shopper the disappearance of the familiar is always unsettling. This at least partially explains the nostalgia people feel when remembering a time when things were different.

Today's Crocker Park and Legacy Village "life style centers" illustrate that developers understand how the power of nostalgia can be commercially translated into "new" shopping formats.

Richman Brothers, a local company established in 1903, with its main factory on East 55th Street, was a major provider of men's clothing. It was purchased by the Woolworth Company in 1968, remaining in business until 1992. In 1937 its newly renovated store at 736 Euclid Avenue attracts a couple window shoppers.
(Cleveland Picture Collection of Cleveland Public Library)

The Burrow Brothers Company, founded in 1873, operated a large chain of stores offering books and office products. Its main store in 1938 was at Euclid Avenue and East Sixth Street. After being purchased by library and school supplier Brodart in 1988, Burrow's remained in business only until 1992.
(Cleveland Picture Collection of Cleveland Public Library)

The main Burrow's store on Euclid Avenue was decorated for Christmas 1938. Books are shelved along the left side of the store, greeting cards and office products to the right.
(Cleveland Picture Collection of Cleveland Public Library)

The S. S. Kresge Company's main downtown store was located on Euclid Avenue at East Fourth Street. Built in 1923 on the site of the old Cleveland Opera House, the store was the largest Kresge outlet in the country. Eventually the "dime store" model of merchandising gave way to the big box K-Mart type stores. Seen here in 1935, the building is now home to the Corner Alley. *(Cleveland Picture Collection of Cleveland Public Library)*

The F. W. Woolworth Company, another major "five and dime" store chain, built a new downtown facility on Euclid Avenue just west of East Fourth Street in 1950. To its right can be seen a portion of the W. T. Grant variety store. The Woolworth store remained in business until 1997. The building was then completely renovated and is now the home of the House of Blues. *(Cleveland Picture Collection of Cleveland Public Library)*

Newman-Stearns (Paul Newman was part of this Newman family) was Cleveland's largest purveyor of sporting goods.
Located on East 12trh Street and Walnut Avenue, in 1967 the store site was claimed for the Erieview Urban Renewal project.
Its site is now the location of the Chester Commons downtown park.
(Cleveland Press *Collection of the Cleveland State University Michael Schwartz Library*)

When it came to Christmas decorations, nothing in the city could rival the downtown department stores' extravagant holiday displays. The May Company, seen here in 1952, promised shoppers "the magic of Christmas at May's." It may not have been magic, but its effect truly was magical.
(Cleveland Picture Collection of Cleveland Public Library)